MORE Improving Comprehension

for ages 9-10

A & C Black • London

Contents

Each text has three comprehension exercises to enable teachers to differentiate across the ability range.

Introduction

Following the success of the Improving Comprehension series, *More Improving Comprehension* provides a further range of interesting and exciting texts for sharing with pupils. The texts have been carefully selected to be appropriate to the age group and to cover a range of text types. The accompanying comprehension worksheets are differentiated at three levels and are designed to be used by individuals or small groups. **Notes for teachers** at the foot of each worksheet provide guidance on how to get the most from the texts and how to approach the questions on the sheet.

For monitoring and recording purposes, an **Individual Record Sheet** is provided on page 4 detailing reading and writing levels appropriate for Year 5. You may find it helpful to make indicative assessments of pupils' levels in both reading and writing by considering their responses to the comprehension exercises.

How to use the book and CD-ROM together

The book has fifteen texts, which can be projected on to a whiteboard for whole class use from the CD-ROM, or photocopied/printed for use with small groups or individuals. Sharing the text either on screen or paper provides lots of opportunities for speaking and listening, for decoding words through a phonic approach, for reading and re-reading for meaning, and for satisfaction and enjoyment in shared success.

For each text there are three comprehension worksheets at different ability levels to enable teachers to differentiate across the ability range. An animal picture at the top of the sheet indicates the level of the worksheet. The cat exercises are at the simplest level; the dog exercises are at the next level; the rabbit exercises are at the most advanced level. You may decide to give some pupils the cat worksheet and then decide, on the basis of their success, to ask them to complete the dog worksheet. A similar approach could be taken with the dog and rabbit sheets.

After reading the text with the pupils, the teacher should discuss the tasks with the children, ensuring that they understand clearly how to complete the worksheet and reminding them to answer the questions using full sentences and correct punctuation.

National Curriculum levels

The worksheets are aimed at the following ability levels:

Cat worksheets are for pupils working towards Level 3.
Dog worksheets are for pupils working at Level 3.
Rabbit worksheets are for pupils who are working confidently at Level 4.

Individual record sheet

Pupil's name: _____

Date of birth: _____

Reading Level 3

☐ I can read a range of texts fluently and accurately.
☐ I can read independently.
☐ I use strategies appropriately to establish meaning.
☐ In my responses to fiction I show understanding of the main points and I express preferences.
☐ In my responses to non-fiction I show understanding of the main points and I express preferences.
☐ I know the order of the alphabet.
☐ I use my knowledge of the alphabet to locate books and find information.

Reading Level 4

☐ I can respond to a range of texts.
☐ I show understanding of significant ideas, themes, events and characters.
☐ I am beginning to use inference and deduction.
☐ I refer to the text when explaining my views.
☐ I can locate and use ideas and information.

Writing Level 3

☐ My writing is often organised, imaginative and clear.
☐ I use the main features of different forms of writing.
☐ I am beginning to adapt my writing to different readers.
☐ I use sequences of sentences to extend ideas logically.
☐ I choose words for variety and interest.
☐ The basic grammatical structure of my sentences is usually correct.
☐ My spelling is usually accurate, including that of common, polysyllabic words.
☐ I use punctuation accurately to mark sentences, including full stops, capital letters and question marks.
☐ My handwriting is joined and legible.

Writing Level 4

☐ I can write in a range of forms.
☐ My writing is lively and thoughtful.
☐ My ideas are often sustained and developed in interesting ways.
☐ My ideas are often organised appropriately for the purpose of the reader.
☐ My choice of vocabulary is often adventurous.
☐ I use words for effect.
☐ I am beginning to use grammatically complex sentences to extend meaning.
☐ My spelling, including that of polysyllabic words that conform to regular patterns, is generally accurate.
☐ I use full stops, capital letters and question marks correctly.
☐ I am beginning to use punctuation within the sentence.
☐ My handwriting is fluent, joined and legible.

Harry hurries home

The owners of Harry, a large black and white cat, are very glad to have him back safe and sound after he had been missing for over three weeks.

George and Emma Jenkins moved to their new house at the end of June and took Harry with them. At first all went well but suddenly Harry disappeared.

"He seemed quite happy at the new house," said George, "but after a few days he went missing. We were really worried about him when he didn't come home one night. I took the next day off work in the hope that he would turn up but he didn't."

"We actually felt quite lonely without him!" said Emma. "For the first few days we were still putting out food for him every morning and clearing it away every evening."

After a couple of weeks, George and Emma had given up hope and they began to get used to life without Harry. "We really thought we'd never see him again," said Emma.

It was an incredible surprise for the couple when they received a phone call from Sally Barton. "Sally's call came completely out of the blue," said George. "She told us that Harry had popped in through the cat-flap!"

"Of course, what Harry had done was find his way all the way back to our old house over a hundred miles away! It took us about two hours in the car to go and fetch him so goodness knows how he made the journey. Harry's amazing!" added Emma, giving Harry a big cuddle.

It remains a mystery how Harry found his way back to his old home in Somerset from his new home in Wiltshire. George and Emma are hoping that he will stay with them from now on but if he doesn't, at least they will know where to look.

Harry hurries home

1 What type of animal is Harry?

_____

_____

2 Who are Harry's owners?

_____

_____

3 For how long was Harry missing?

_____

_____

4 Where had Harry gone?

_____

_____

5 How many miles away had Harry gone?

_____

_____

6 Write a summary of Harry's story.

_____

_____

_____

_____

_____

Notes for teachers
Help the children to read the passage slowly and carefully, ensuring that they understand the story. Discuss the questions with them and encourage them to work out their answers orally before putting anything down on paper. Do they remember to write in complete sentences, using appropriate punctuation? The final question is very challenging but discuss ideas with the children.

Name: _____   Date: _____

Harry hurries home

1 What does Harry look like?

_____

_____

2 In which county did Harry and his owners live before they moved
   house?

_____

_____

3 Which county did Harry and his owners move to?

_____

_____

4 Describe how Harry's owners felt when he was missing.

_____

_____

5 How did Harry's owners find him again?

_____

_____

6 Write about a pet that does something special.

_____

_____

_____

_____

_____

Notes for teachers
Help the children to read the passage carefully, ensuring that they understand the story. Discuss the questions with
them and encourage them to work out their answers orally before putting anything down on paper. Do they remember
to write in complete sentences, using appropriate punctuation? The final question is very challenging but discuss ideas
with the children. In answer to this question they could choose to write a summary of Harry's story.

Harry hurries home

Write the script for a radio or television programme where Harry's owners are interviewed about Harry's adventure.

_____

_____

_____

_____

_____

_____

_____

_____

_____

_____

_____

_____

_____

_____

_____

_____

_____

_____

_____

_____

_____

_____

Notes for teachers
Ensure that the pupils have read and understand the story. Talk about the activity. Encourage them to consider the types of questions that Harry's owners could be asked by a radio or TV presenter. They may wish to act out the programme.

 Andrew Brodie: More Improving Comprehension for Ages 9–10 © A&C Black, Bloomsbury Publishing 2012

Thank you letter

23 Saffron Walk,
Stratton St Paul,
Swindon,
Wiltshire.
SN14 2QR

27th July 2012

Dear Sally,

George and I would like to express our sincere gratitude to you for looking after Harry when he made his own way back to Somerset! He has always been quite an adventurous cat but this is the biggest adventure he has ever undertaken.

We had a good journey back to Swindon with Harry safely contained in a cat basket. He didn't like it very much. He was yowling the whole way but we knew it was the best thing for him.

We hope you are enjoying living in the house as much as we did. We are so pleased that you still had the cat-flap so that Harry could find his way in.

Our new house is very nice but we do miss being in Somerset. Do call in and see us if you are ever over this way.

Best wishes,

Emma

Thank you letter

1   Who wrote the letter?

_____

_____

2   Why did she write the letter?

_____

_____

3   What village does she live in?

_____

_____

4   What is the number of her house?

_____

_____

5   What is her postcode?

_____

_____

6   Write your home address very carefully, as though you are writing it
     at the top of a letter.

_____

_____

_____

_____

_____

_____

Notes for teachers
Help the children to read the letter, ensuring that they understand who it is from and who it is to. Discuss the questions
with them and encourage them to work out their answers orally before putting anything down on paper. Encourage
them to answer the questions fully – for example, the answer to the first question could simply be 'Emma' but the
children could add more detail such as the fact that she is the owner of the cat. Do they remember to write in complete
sentences, using appropriate punctuation?

Thank you letter

1 Who was the letter from?

_____

_____

2 Which words did Emma use to say thank you?

_____

_____

3 What road does she live in?

_____

_____

4 What is her postal town?

_____

_____

5 How did Harry travel back to Swindon?

_____

_____

6 Write your school address very carefully, as though you are writing it at the top of a letter.

_____

_____

_____

_____

_____

_____

Notes for teachers

Help the children to read the letter, ensuring that they understand who it is from and who it is to. Discuss the questions with them and encourage them to work out their answers orally before putting anything down on paper. Encourage them to answer the questions fully. Note that the answer to the first question may not simply be the writer herself. Do they remember to write in complete sentences, using appropriate punctuation?

Name: _____ **Date:** _____

Thank you letter

1   Why did Emma write the letter?

_____

_____

2   Write a short description of Harry.

_____

_____

_____

_____

3   How do you think Emma feels about having moved house? What evidence can you find for your answer?

_____

_____

_____

4   Emma signs off her letter by writing 'best wishes' before her name. Which other words or phrases could she have used?

_____

_____

5   Make up an imaginary address and write it very carefully, as though you are writing it at the top of a letter.

_____

_____

_____

_____

_____

Notes for teachers

Help the children to read the letter, ensuring that they understand who it is from and who it is to. They may wish to look back at the passage 'Harry hurries home' to help them with some of the questions. Encourage them to answer the questions fully. Do they remember to write in complete sentences, using appropriate punctuation?

   Andrew Brodie: More Improving Comprehension for Ages 9–10 © A&C Black, Bloomsbury Publishing 2012

Letter of complaint

24 Saffron Walk,
Stratton St Paul,
Swindon,
Wiltshire.
SN14 2QR

3rd September 2012

Dear Mr and Mrs Jenkins,

I am very sorry to have to write this letter to you but my wife and I have had as much as we can take.

The noise that cat makes every night is keeping us awake. Not only that, it comes in our garden and digs holes and it chases our Alsatian and eats his food. It also scratches the wooden supports of our porch and makes marks on them so that I have had to repaint them twice since you moved in.

Our previous neighbours, Frank and Connie, were very good friends of ours. Just like you, they had a cat but it never caused us any trouble. If the problems continue, we will have no choice but to contact the council.

We look forward to your reply.

Yours sincerely,
        Mr C J Moaner

Letter of complaint

1 Who wrote the letter?

_____

_____

2 Who did he write the letter to?

_____

_____

3 What was he complaining about?

_____

_____

4 When did he write the letter?

_____

_____

5 What pet does he have?

_____

_____

6 Who were the previous neighbours to Mr and Mrs Moaner?

_____

_____

Notes for teachers
This activity should be approached after the pupils have completed the previous two activities in the book. Help the children to read the letter, ensuring that they understand who it is from and who it is to. Discuss the questions with them and encourage them to work out their answers orally before putting anything down on paper. Encourage them to answer the questions fully. Do they remember to write in complete sentences, using appropriate punctuation?

Letter of complaint

1   How close to Mr and Mrs Jenkins did Mr and Mrs Moaner live, do you think? How do you know this?

_____

_____

_____

2   What or who exactly is causing the problems to Mr and Mrs Moaner?

_____

_____

3   What problems are being caused?

_____

_____

_____

4   What is Mr Moaner going to do if the problems continue?

_____

_____

5   How do you think that Mr and Mrs Jenkins could solve the problems?

_____

_____

_____

6   What is the very first thing Mr and Mrs Jenkins should do?

_____

_____

Notes for teachers
This activity should be approached after the pupils have completed the previous two activities in the book. Help the children to read the letter, ensuring that they understand who it is from and who it is to. Encourage them to answer the questions fully. Do they remember to write in complete sentences, using appropriate punctuation?

Letter of complaint

1 Why did Mr Moaner write the letter?

_____

_____

2 What are the five things that Mr Moaner is blaming the cat for?

_____

_____

_____

_____

_____

3 Why does Mr Moaner mention his previous neighbours?

_____

_____

_____

_____

4 What is the first thing that Mr Moaner is expecting from Mr and Mrs Jenkins?

_____

_____

5 Imagine that you are Mr or Mrs Jenkins. Write a reply to Mr Moaner. **Jot down some ideas on the lines below then use a clean piece of paper to write your letter.**

_____

_____

_____

_____

_____

Notes for teachers
This activity should be approached after the pupils have completed the previous two activities in the book. Help the children to read the letter, ensuring that they understand who it is from and who it is to. Encourage them to answer the questions fully. Do they remember to write in complete sentences, using appropriate punctuation?

It's snowing

Character A is looking out of the window excitedly. Character B is unexcited throughout, until receiving the best news at the end!

A Wow! It's snowing!

B Oh, no!

A What do you mean 'oh no'?

B Well, it's going to cause so much trouble. All the roads will be closed.

A Oh, I'm so excited! We can go outside and play snowballs.

B I hate snowballs. The snow always goes down your neck.

A Quick, put your scarf on then. Let's get our wellies on!

B Oh, not my wellies. They're so cold in the snow and my toes freeze. They feel like they're going to drop off.

A *(ignoring B)* Oh, look at it! It's coming down really fast now. Look at those great big flakes!

B The only flakes I like are Cadburys!

A It's so exciting! We'll build a great snowman.

B That means picking up the snow in your hands and my fingers freeze. They feel like they're going to drop off.

A Put your gloves on then. *(A pauses and looks worried)* The only big problem is …

B Oh, no, I knew there'd be a big problem!

A … we're going to have to miss school.

B Why?

A School is closed because of the snow. *(A looks really upset)*

B *(B's face brightens up)* Yippee! Let's go out and play in it!

It's snowing

1 What type of passage is this?

_____

_____

2 Who is pleased that it's snowing?

_____

_____

3 Who is not pleased that it's snowing?

_____

_____

4 Why does Character B not like snowballs?

_____

_____

5 Does Character B like snowflakes?

_____

_____

6 Write about how you feel when it's snowing.

_____

_____

_____

_____

_____

Notes for teachers
Help the children to read the passage, ensuring that they understand that it is the script for a short play. If possible, the children could act out the play, taking turns to be Character A or Character B. Discuss the questions with them and encourage them to work out their answers orally before putting anything down on paper. Do they remember to write in complete sentences, using appropriate punctuation? Encourage them to write more than one word in reply to question 5 – this is an important skill.

It's snowing

1 Why is Character A pleased that it's snowing?

_____

_____

2 Give two of the reasons Character B is not pleased about the snow.

_____

_____

_____

3 What does Character A suggest as a solution to the problem of snow going down Character B's neck?

_____

_____

4 What big problem does Character A think of?

_____

_____

5 How does Character B respond to that problem?

_____

_____

6 What do you think is good about snowy weather and what do you think is bad about snowy weather?

_____

_____

_____

_____

_____

Notes for teachers
Ensure that the children understand that this passage is the script for a short play. If possible, the children could act out the play, taking turns to be Character A or Character B. Do they remember to write in complete sentences, using appropriate punctuation?

It's snowing

1 Why do you think the writer has chosen to call the characters A and B, rather than using names for them?

_____

_____

2 What aspects of the snowy weather does Character A find exciting?

_____

_____

_____

_____

3 What aspects of the snowy weather does Character B not like?

_____

_____

_____

_____

4 Which one aspect of the weather is Character B pleased about?

_____

_____

5 Choose Character A or Character B. What do you think your chosen character is like? Write a short description.

_____

_____

_____

_____

_____

Notes for teachers
Ensure that the children understand that this passage is the script for a short play. If possible the children could act out the play, taking turns to be Character A or Character B, who, as they are not named, can be acted by boys or girls. Do they remember to write in complete sentences, using appropriate punctuation?

Winter morning

Winter is the king of showmen,
Turning tree stumps into snowmen
And houses into birthday cakes
And spreading sugar over lakes.
Smooth and clean and frosty white,
The world looks good enough to bite.
That's the season to be young,
Catching snowflakes on your tongue.

Snow is snowy when it's snowing,
I'm sorry it's slushy when it's going.

by Ogden Nash

Name: _____ Date: _____

Winter morning

1 What word in the poem rhymes with cakes?

_____

_____

2 What word in the poem rhymes with bite?

_____

_____

3 What does the writer describe as a king?

_____

_____

4 What do the lakes look like?

_____

_____

5 What does the writer not like?

_____

_____

6 Write about today's weather. What is it like?

_____

_____

_____

_____

Notes for teachers
Ask the children to read the poem, supporting them with any tricky words. Discuss it with them, encouraging them to understand the descriptions – the writer makes great use of metaphors, which some children will not understand without help. Discuss the questions with them and encourage them to work out their answers orally before putting anything down on paper. Do they remember to write in complete sentences, using appropriate punctuation?

  Andrew Brodie: More Improving Comprehension for Ages 9–10 © A&C Black, Bloomsbury Publishing 2012

Winter morning

1   What word in the poem rhymes with snowing?

_____

_____

2   What word in the poem rhymes with tongue?

_____

_____

3   Why do the houses look like birthday cakes?

_____

_____

4   Why does the world look good enough to bite?

_____

_____

5   Is there really sugar on the lakes? What does the writer mean?

_____

_____

6   Write about today's weather. What is it like? Can you make a rhyming verse about it?

_____

_____

_____

_____

_____

Notes for teachers
Ask the children to read the poem. Discuss it with them, encouraging them to understand the descriptions – the writer makes great use of metaphors, which some children will not understand without help. Discuss the questions with them and encourage them to work out their answers orally before putting anything down on paper. Do they remember to write in complete sentences, using appropriate punctuation?

Winter morning

1   Why is winter a good season to be young?

_____

_____

_____

2   Why might winter not be a good season to be old?

_____

_____

_____

3   What effect of winter makes the tree stumps look like snowmen?

_____

_____

4   What is a showman, do you think?

_____

_____

5   Why is winter the *king* of showmen?

_____

_____

6   Write about your favourite weather. Can you make a rhyming verse about it?

_____

_____

_____

_____

_____

Notes for teachers
Ask the children to read the poem. Discuss it with them, encouraging them to understand the descriptions – the writer makes great use of metaphors, which some children will not understand without help. Discuss the questions with them and encourage them to work out their answers orally before putting anything down on paper. Do they remember to write in complete sentences, using appropriate punctuation?

     Andrew Brodie: More Improving Comprehension for Ages 9–10 © A&C Black, Bloomsbury Publishing 2012

Counter-Feet

The following extract is from the book Septimus Heap, Flyte by Angie Sage.
In this passage, two people are meeting to play a rather special board game
called Counter-Feet.

At first sight the game appeared to be a simple board game played with Counters.
The Counter-Feet board consisted of two castles divided by a river down the
centre. Each player had a set of Counters of various shapes and sizes in their
own team strip, and the aim of the game was to get as many of your own
Counters over the river and into the opposing player's castle. But there was a
twist in the game: the Counters had minds of their own – and, more importantly,
feet of their own.

This was why the game was so popular, but unfortunately this was also the
reason for the game's rarity. The Charms that created the Counters had been lost
in The Great Fire three hundred years ago. And since then, most sets of Counter-
Feet had gradually become incomplete as over the years their Counters had up
and left in search of adventure or just in search of a more interesting box of
Counter-Feet. And while no one ever objected to opening his or her box and
finding that a whole new colony of Counters had taken up residence, it was a
different matter when you discovered that all your Counters had got bored with
you and left. So three hundred years later, most Counters had disappeared:
flushed down drains, trodden into the ground or simply having a good time in
small, undiscovered Counter colonies under the floor-boards.

Most Wizards, including Silas, played the Magyk version of Counter-Feet,
where the castles and the river on the board were real – although smaller of
course. Ever since he was a boy, Gringe had always wanted to play with a
Magyk set of Counter-Feet. When Silas had mentioned to Gringe that he actually
had a complete and sealed Magyk Counter-Feet set somewhere in the attic with
all his books, Gringe had miraculously overcome his long-standing dislike of the
Heap family and suggested that they might, perhaps, have a game or two
together sometime. It had soon become a regular occurrence which both looked
forward to.

Counter-Feet

1   What game is about to be played?

_____

_____

2   What was on each side of the game board?

_____

_____

3   What ran down the middle of the board?

_____

_____

4   Which two people are playing the game?

_____

_____

5   What two things were special about the Counters?

_____

_____

6   Write about a board game you have played. What does the board
    look like?

_____

_____

_____

_____

_____

Notes for teachers
Help the children to read the passage slowly and carefully. The story is very complex but the concept is amusing to children once they understand it. Discuss the questions with them and encourage them to work out their answers orally before putting anything down on paper. Do they remember to write in complete sentences, using appropriate punctuation?

   Andrew Brodie: More Improving Comprehension for Ages 9–10 © A&C Black, Bloomsbury Publishing 2012

Counter-Feet

1 What book does this passage come from?

_____

_____

2 What was the game board like?

_____

_____

3 What did the Charms do?

_____

_____

4 What had happened to the Charms?

_____

_____

5 What was special about the Magyk version of the game?

_____

_____

6 Write about a board game you have played. What does the board look like? How many people play the game? How do you win the game?

_____

_____

_____

_____

_____

Notes for teachers
Help the children to read the passage slowly and carefully. The story is very complex but the concept is amusing to children once they understand it. Discuss the questions with them and encourage them to work out their answers orally before putting anything down on paper. Do they remember to write in complete sentences, using appropriate punctuation?

Counter-Feet

1   Who is the author of this passage?

_____

_____

2   What special feature made the game popular?

_____

_____

3   Why had some Counters left their own box of Counter-feet?

_____

_____

4   Why were most sets of the game now incomplete?

_____

_____

5   Why might Gringe have not wanted to play against Silas Heap?

_____

_____

6   Imagine a game that you could create. What would the board look
    like? How many people could play the game at any one time? How
    could a person win the game?

_____

_____

_____

_____

_____

Notes for teachers
Help the children to read the passage slowly and carefully. The story is very complex but the concept is amusing to
children once they understand it. Do they remember to write in complete sentences, using appropriate punctuation?
The final question is very challenging but the passage may give pupils some ideas.

   Andrew Brodie: More Improving Comprehension for Ages 9–10 © A&C Black, Bloomsbury Publishing 2012

Holiday cottage

- Come and stay at our beautiful holiday cottage, deep in the heart of the Somerset countryside. Willow Barn has been converted to offer four-star accommodation and is within easy reach of the M5 motorway.

- The front of the cottage opens on to the farmyard here at Tayton Farm. The garden rises alongside the cottage and there is an acre of lawn behind it. The main patio faces south and has wonderful views of the Blackdown Hills.

- The accommodation features two large bedrooms, one of which has an en-suite shower room. There is also a separate bathroom. The open-plan living area has a fitted kitchen, dining area and spacious lounge with open beams. The two sets of patio doors lead to the huge garden and provide excellent views of the surrounding countryside.

- The cottage has full oil-fired central heating and the efficient system provides a constant supply of hot water. Basic essentials, such as washing up liquid, salt, pepper, sugar, tea-bags and coffee will all be available. Bedding will be supplied.

- Willow Barn makes an excellent base for exploring the Quantock Hills, Exmoor and the whole of Somerset. Devon is only a couple of miles away and beaches can be reached in just 45 minutes. A network of public footpaths can be found in the immediate locality. The small town of Wellington is nearby and the county town of Taunton is approximately nine miles away.

We look forward to hearing from you.

Holiday cottage

1   What type of passage is this?

_____

_____

2   In which county is the holiday cottage?

_____

_____

3   What is the holiday cottage called?

_____

_____

4   What is the main feature of the garden?

_____

_____

5   Which town is near to the cottage?

_____

_____

6   Write about a place you have visited during a school holiday.

_____

_____

_____

_____

_____

Notes for teachers

Help the children to read the passage slowly and carefully, ensuring that they understand that it is an advertisement for a holiday cottage. Discuss the questions with them and encourage them to work out their answers orally before putting anything down on paper. Do they remember to write in complete sentences, using appropriate punctuation? Note that question 6 allows for the pupils to write about a place visited for just a day or for a longer holiday.

Holiday cottage

1   What is being advertised?

_____

_____

2   Where is the holiday cottage?

_____

_____

3   What is special about one of the bedrooms?

_____

_____

4   Why would the cottage be suitable for visiting in the winter as well as in the summer?

_____

_____

5   Which county is nearby?

_____

_____

6   Write about a place where you would like to have a holiday.

_____

_____

_____

_____

_____

Notes for teachers
Ensure that the children understand that the passage is an advertisement for a holiday cottage. Discuss the questions with them and encourage them to work out their answers orally before putting anything down on paper. Do they remember to write in complete sentences, using appropriate punctuation? Note that question 6 allows for the pupils to write about a place they have visited before or about somewhere they would like to go.

Holiday cottage

1 What does 'en-suite' mean?

_____

_____

2 Which two ranges of hills are mentioned in the advertisement?

_____

_____

3 What could people do when staying at the cottage?

_____

_____

_____

_____

_____

4 Why is facing south an advantage?

_____

_____

5 Write about a place near to you, which would be suitable for holiday visitors. What is interesting about it?

_____

_____

_____

_____

_____

Notes for teachers
Ensure that the children understand that the passage is an advertisement for a holiday cottage. Discuss the questions with them and encourage them to work out their answers orally before putting anything down on paper. Do they remember to write in complete sentences, using appropriate punctuation?

September the third

The extract below is taken from The Dragonfly Pool by Eva Ibbotson.

Nobody ever forgot where they were on the day that war was declared.

Tally was in the kitchen helping Aunt May to prepare the vegetables for Sunday lunch when the music on the wireless stopped and the announcer said that the Prime Minister would address the nation at eleven o'clock. Everyone had been expecting it; Hitler had invaded Poland two days before and the democratic countries had had enough. Aunt Hester came hurrying in from the garden and Tally's father from his study.

The Prime Minister was old and tired; he had tried to keep the peace and now he told the people of Great Britain that he had failed. An ultimatum had been sent to Hitler demanding that he withdraw his troops from Poland.

'I have to tell you that no such undertaking has been received and that consequently this country is at war with Germany.'

No one ever forgot what happened next either. Almost straight away the air-raid sirens sounded – that hideous wailing that they had only just learned to recognize.

'Quick, into the shelter,' said Dr Hamilton, pushing his daughter towards the door.

'Oh dear, my roast will be spoiled – couldn't you go ahead, and let me –' began Aunt May, and saw her brother's face.

The shelter was at the bottom of the street. It was not really finished yet and a puddle of water had collected in the bottom. The lady from number 4 said she wasn't going down into that wetness, she'd rather be bombed than die of pneumonia. She was a very large person and the people behind her got nasty because she was blocking the door.

They had just climbed down when the all-clear went. It had been a false alarm.

Name: _____ Date: _____

September the third

1 What was special about September the third?

_____

_____

_____

2 Who was in the kitchen?

_____

_____

3 What relation is Dr Hamilton to Tally?

_____

_____

4 Where was the air-raid shelter?

_____

_____

5 What was wrong with the air-raid shelter?

_____

_____

6 What happened once everyone was in the air-raid shelter?

_____

_____

_____

Notes for teachers
Help the children to read the passage slowly and carefully, ensuring that they understand the story. Discuss the questions with them and encourage them to work out their answers orally before putting anything down on paper. Do they remember to write in complete sentences, using appropriate punctuation?

 Andrew Brodie: More Improving Comprehension for Ages 9–10 © A&C Black, Bloomsbury Publishing 2012

September the third

1 What book is the passage taken from?

_____

_____

2 What is a wireless?

_____

_____

3 Which of Tally's relations are mentioned in the passage?

_____

_____

4 At what time did the announcement of the start of the war take place?

_____

_____

5 What did the air-raid warning sound like?

_____

_____

6 Describe how you would feel if you had been in Tally's house on that day.

_____

_____

_____

_____

_____

Notes for teachers
Ask the children to read the passage carefully, ensuring that they understand the story. Discuss the questions with them and encourage them to work out their answers orally before putting anything down on paper. Do they remember to write in complete sentences, using appropriate punctuation?

Andrew Brodie: More Improving Comprehension for Ages 9–10 © A&C Black, Bloomsbury Publishing 2012

September the third

1 Who is the author of this passage?

_____

_____

2 Why do you think nobody ever forgot where they were on the day that war was declared?

_____

_____

3 In what year is the story set?

_____

_____

4 Think about **every** person who is mentioned in the passage. How do you think each one felt on the day that war was declared?

_____

_____

_____

_____

_____

_____

_____

_____

_____

_____

_____

Notes for teachers
Ask the children to read the story then check that they understand it. Discuss the questions with them and encourage them to work out their answers orally before putting anything down on paper. Do they remember to write in complete sentences, using appropriate punctuation?

 Andrew Brodie: More Improving Comprehension for Ages 9–10 © A&C Black, Bloomsbury Publishing 2012

Eva Ibbotson

Eva Ibbotson wrote The Dragonfly Pool and many other novels.

Eva Ibbotson was born in Austria on 21st January 1925. At that stage of her life her name was not Eva at all: she was called Maria Charlotte Michelle Wiesner.

Her parents separated when she was very young so Eva spent most of her time at her grandmother's house. When she was eight years old Eva moved to Edinburgh in Scotland to join her father. She didn't stay with him for very long before moving to London to live with her mother in 1934.

Eva was sent away to boarding school. She loved her time at Dartington Hall School, set in the countryside of Devon. When she grew up she went to university in London and Cambridge. She met a young man called Alan Ibbotson and they married in 1947.

The couple lived in Bristol then Newcastle and they had four children. Eva trained to become a teacher and she began to write short stories. Her first full-length book was called The Great Ghost Rescue. Although it was published in 1975 it was not until thirty-six years later that it came out as a film.

Eva was the author of many books for adults as well as for children. Her adult books are very popular in Germany but in this country she is better known for her children's books. Her titles include Journey to the River Sea, The Secret of Platform 13, The Dragonfly Pool and The Star of Kazan.

Eva Ibbotson died on 20th October 2010 at the age of 85.

Eva Ibbotson

Ring the correct answer for each of the following three questions.

1   The word nearest in meaning to 'author' is:

editor   writer   reader   publisher

2   The word nearest in meaning to 'loved' is:

enjoyed   hated   respected   trained

3   The word nearest in meaning to 'began' is:

begun   beginning   starting   started

Write full sentences to answer these questions.

4   In what year was Eva born?

_____

_____

5   In what county did Eva go to school?

_____

_____

6   Give the titles of two of the books that Eva wrote.

_____

_____

_____

Notes for teachers
Help the children to read the passage slowly and carefully, ensuring that they understand that it is a biography. For each of the first three questions encourage them to find the word that is most relevant to the passage.

Andrew Brodie: More Improving Comprehension for Ages 9–10 © A&C Black, Bloomsbury Publishing 2012

Eva Ibbotson

Ring the correct answer for each of the following three questions.

1   The word nearest in meaning to 'stage' is:

theatre   performance   part   platform

2   The word nearest in meaning to 'trained' is:

taught   learned   advised   repeated

3   The word nearest in meaning to 'full-length' is:

completing   completed   complete   completion

Write full sentences to answer these questions.

4   How old was Eva when she went to live with her mother?

_____

_____

5   Which school did Eva attend?

_____

_____

6   Give the titles of five of the books that Eva wrote.

_____

_____

_____

Notes for teachers
Ask the children to read the passage carefully, ensuring that they understand that it is a biography. For each of the first three questions encourage them to find the word that is most relevant to the passage. For example, for the first question the pupils could be tempted to choose 'theatre' or 'platform' but the word most relevant to the context would be 'part'.

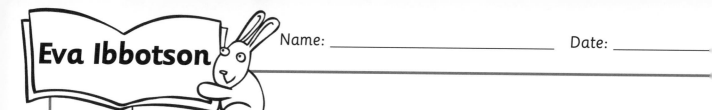

Ring the correct answer for each of the following three questions.

1   The word nearest in meaning to 'called' is:

named   shouted   beckoned   summoned

2   The word nearest in meaning to 'set' is:

group   imposed   situated   given

3   The word nearest in meaning to 'published' is:

released   written   recorded   filmed

Write full sentences to answer these questions.

4   Which of Eva's books were more popular in Germany?

_____

_____

5   In what year did the film of The Great Ghost Rescue come out?

_____

_____

6   Write a brief description of a book you have read, including who wrote it.

_____

_____

_____

_____

_____

Notes for teachers

Ask the children to read the passage carefully, ensuring that they understand that it is a biography. For each of the first three questions encourage them to find the word that is most relevant to the passage. For example, for the first question the pupils could be tempted to choose 'shouted' but the word most relevant to the context would be 'named'.

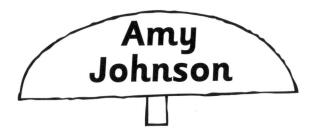

Amy Johnson

Amy Johnson was a famous pilot during the 1930s.

Amy Johnson was born on 1st July 1903. As a young woman she had an ambition to fly aeroplanes. She had a job as a secretary but in her spare time she learnt how to fly. When she was twenty-six years old she gained her licence as a pilot.

Amy was lucky because her father helped her to buy a second-hand aeroplane. She was very excited when she bought an aeroplane called a Gipsy Moth. She named her aeroplane 'Jason'! In 1930 she flew Jason all on her own from England to Australia. It took her nineteen days to make the journey from Croydon to Darwin, a distance of eleven thousand miles, or eighteen thousand kilometres. When she arrived in Australia she was welcomed by crowds of people.

After her success in flying to Australia, Amy became a famous celebrity all over the world. She went on to make many record-breaking flights.

The Second World War broke out in September 1939. In 1940, Amy was able to join the Air Transport Auxiliary. Her job was to deliver aeroplanes from the factories where they were made to the airfields from which they would fly into combat.

During the delivery of an aircraft from Blackpool to Oxford on 5th January 1941, the weather conditions became very poor. Amy was unable to see the ground to find her route. She bailed out of the aircraft over the Thames Estuary and was drowned.

If you would like to see Amy Johnson's aeroplane, 'Jason', it is on display in the Flight Gallery at the Science Museum in London.

Amy Johnson

Ring the correct answer for each of the following three questions.

1   The word nearest in meaning to 'spare' is:

free   hobby   loan   learn

2   The word nearest in meaning to 'journey' is:

journeyed   tripped   trip   journal

3   The word nearest in meaning to 'well-known' is:

famous   celebrated   celebrity   celebration

Write full sentences to answer these questions.

4   In what year was Amy born?

_____

_____

5   What did she call her aeroplane?

_____

_____

6   What was Amy's job during the war?

_____

_____

_____

Notes for teachers

Help the children to read the passage slowly and carefully, ensuring that they understand that it is a biography. For each of the first three questions encourage them to find the word that is most relevant to the passage. Discuss the words with them – can they explain what each alternative word means?

Amy Johnson

Ring the correct answer for each of the following three questions.

1   The word nearest in meaning to 'helped' is:

assisted   supported   repaired   fixed

2   The word nearest in meaning to 'deliver' is:

post   receive   take   took

3   The word opposite in meaning to 'success' is:

victory   win   failing   failure

Write full sentences to answer these questions.

4   How old was Amy when the Second World War started?

_____

_____

5   Which organisation did Amy join in the war?

_____

_____

6   In what way was Amy lucky and in what way was she unlucky?

_____

_____

_____

_____

Notes for teachers
Ask the children to read the passage carefully, ensuring that they understand that it is a biography. For each of the first three questions encourage them to find the word that is most relevant to the passage. Discuss the words with them – can they explain what each alternative word means? The pupils may need to discuss ideas to answer the final question.

Amy Johnson

Ring the correct answer for each of the following three questions.

1 The word nearest in meaning to 'ambition' is:

   desire   requirement   demand   involvement

2 The word nearest in meaning to 'broke out' is:

   commencement   start   escaped   commenced

3 The word opposite in meaning to 'helped' is:

   supported   prevented   destroyed   deployed

Write full sentences to answer these questions.

4 Which town in Australia did Amy reach?

   _____

   _____

5 Find out about another famous pilot. Write a short biography of your chosen pilot.

   _____

   _____

   _____

   _____

   _____

   _____

   _____

   _____

Notes for teachers

Ask the children to read the passage carefully, ensuring that they understand that it is a biography. For each of the first three questions encourage them to find the word that is most relevant to the passage. Discuss the words with them – can they explain what each alternative word means? Help the pupils to research information for the final question.

     Andrew Brodie: More Improving Comprehension for Ages 9–10 © A&C Black, Bloomsbury Publishing 2012

At the airport

Although lots of his friends have been on aeroplanes before, Tom has never travelled anywhere by air. He was so excited about his first flight that he wrote down in his diary exactly what happened.

Once we had parked we walked in though the big glass doors of the airport. There were lots of people standing in lots of queues so we had to find the right queue to stand in.

The first thing we had to do was to check in our baggage. I have my own suitcase but it's small enough to fit on the plane so all we had to check in was Mum's great big one. I don't know what she puts in it!

After that we had to queue at the departure gate. When we got to the front of the queue we had to put our plastic water bottles into a big bin. I had to take off my belt and my glasses and I had to take the coins out of my pocket. I had to put all these things in a tray. The tray and my suitcase went along a conveyer belt so they could be checked.

Mum had to put her things in a tray as well, then we had to go through a big metal gate one at a time. I got through all right but the gate bleeped when Mum went through. A lady patted Mum all over then spotted that Mum still had her necklace on so Mum had to take it off and go back through the gate again.

I got my stuff back from the people who checked it. They seemed quite happy with it.

Me and Mum went and had a look in the shops. I wanted to buy a big bag of sweets and we had to show the cashier my boarding pass when I bought it.

I kept checking the flashing signs to see if our plane was due to depart. Suddenly it showed up: Flight to Alicante. Now boarding. Gate 3.

We rushed to Gate 3 but we didn't need to rush because we found another queue! We queued to get on the plane then we found two seats together quite near the front. Mum lifted my suitcase and her hand luggage into the overhead locker.

We were ready to go and I was very excited.

At the airport

Name: _____ Date: _____

1 What was Tom doing for the first time in his life?

_____

_____

2 Who was travelling with Tom?

_____

_____

3 What was the first queue for?

_____

_____

4 In what did Tom and his mum put some of their possessions?

_____

_____

5 What did Tom buy?

_____

_____

6 Write about a time when you went somewhere for the very first time.

_____

_____

_____

_____

_____

Notes for teachers
Help the children to read the passage slowly and carefully, ensuring that they understand the sequence of events. Discuss the questions with them and encourage them to work out their answers orally before putting anything down on paper. Do they remember to write in complete sentences, using appropriate punctuation?

Andrew Brodie: More Improving Comprehension for Ages 9–10 © A&C Black, Bloomsbury Publishing 2012

At the airport

1   In what did Tom write about the visit to the airport?

_____

_____

2   What did Tom and his mum have to find first when they were inside the airport?

_____

_____

3   How was Mum's suitcase different to Tom's?

_____

_____

4   Why did the lady pat Tom's mum all over?

_____

_____

5   Where were Tom and his mum travelling to? Do you know what country that is in?

_____

_____

6   Write about a time when you had to get ready for a journey. Where were you going? What did you pack? Did you need to take anything special?

_____

_____

_____

_____

Notes for teachers
Ask the children to read the passage carefully, ensuring that they understand the sequence of events. Discuss the questions with them and encourage them to work out their answers orally before putting anything down on paper. Do they remember to write in complete sentences, using appropriate punctuation?

At the airport

Name: _____ Date: _____

1 What did Tom and his mum have to put in the bin?

_____

_____

2 Why didn't they have to check in Tom's bag?

_____

_____

3 What type of items did the travellers have to put into trays? Do you know why?

_____

_____

4 Why did Tom's mum have to take off her necklace?

_____

_____

5 How many queues did the travellers have to join? Write a summary of what each queue was for.

_____

_____

_____

6 What is the nearest airport to where you live? Have you ever been there? Give some examples of destinations that can be reached from your local airport.

_____

_____

_____

_____

Notes for teachers
Ask the children to read the passage carefully, ensuring that they understand the sequence of events. Do they remember to write in complete sentences, using appropriate punctuation? The pupils may need some help in researching the final question.

Andrew Brodie: More Improving Comprehension for Ages 9–10 © A&C Black, Bloomsbury Publishing 2012

A tough day

Eddie lay in bed, considering the day ahead of him: School. And the worst thing about school: Mr Tuffman, the new teacher who had arrived at the start of the summer term.

"My name's Tuffman," he had said on his first day. "Tuffman by name, and a tough man by nature. Do you get the idea?"

Eddie certainly hadn't got the idea. Grinning at what he thought was a joke had been a very bad move.

"What's so funny, young man?" Mr Tuffman had said.

All eyes in the class had swivelled towards Eddie. Within seconds, Eddie's eyes had filled like toilet cisterns ready to flush. He didn't know what to say.

"I asked you a question. What do you think is so funny?"

Eddie had remained silent. He tried to answer but actually, now he thought about it, he couldn't see the funny side of it at all. Then the flush happened and tears gushed down his cheeks.

"Pull yourself together, lad. What's your name?" Mr Tuffman had barked the question.

"Eddie," Eddie had replied, wiping his face and his running nose with the sleeve of his school sweatshirt.

"Eddie what?" Mr Tuffman's voice had risen as he had spoken.

"Eddie Smith."

"Eddie Smith what?" Mr Tuffman had asked.

"Just Eddie Smith," Eddie had replied.

"Have you got no manners, Just Eddie Smith? When you answer one of my questions I expect you to say Sir. So, it's not Just Eddie Smith is it? It's Just Eddie Smith, SIR. DO YOU UNDERSTAND ME?"

"Yes."

"Yes what, Just Eddie Smith?"

"Yes, Sir," Eddie had said.

"That's a bit better. Now do you understand what 'tough' means?"

A tough day

1 What was the name of Eddie's teacher?

_____

_____

2 Why did the teacher tell Eddie off?

_____

_____

3 What is Eddie's full name?

_____

_____

4 What did the teacher want Eddie to call him?

_____

_____

5 What did the teacher keep calling Eddie?

_____

_____

6 Write about an imaginary teacher who is kind to you. What is he or she like? How does he or she speak to you?

_____

_____

_____

_____

_____

Notes for teachers

Help the children to read the passage slowly and carefully, ensuring that they understand the story. Discuss the questions with them. Do they remember to write in complete sentences, using appropriate punctuation? It is important that they use their imagination for the last question!

A tough day

1 Why did Eddie grin?

_____

_____

2 When did Mr Tuffman start at the school?

_____

_____

3 When does this story take place?

_____

_____

4 Why do you think everybody looked at Eddie?

_____

_____

5 What were like toilet cisterns?

_____

_____

6 Write about Mr Tuffman. What is he like? How does he speak to Eddie?

_____

_____

_____

_____

_____

Notes for teachers
Ask the children to read the passage carefully, ensuring that they understand the story. Discuss the questions with them. Do they remember to write in complete sentences, using appropriate punctuation? Can they find sufficient evidence in the passage to complete question 6 successfully?

A tough day

1 Why does most of the story appear in italics?

_____

_____

2 Do you think Mr Tuffman likes his own name?

_____

_____

3 Do you think that Mr Tuffman is a tough teacher?

_____

_____

4 Why do you think that some of the passage appears in capital letters?

_____

_____

5 How does Eddie feel about school?

_____

_____

6 Write about an imaginary teacher who starts at your school. What is he or she like? How does he or she speak to you? You must not write about an actual teacher who you already know – use your imagination!

_____

_____

_____

_____

_____

Notes for teachers
Ask the children to read the passage carefully, ensuring that they understand the story. Discuss the questions with them. Do they remember to write in complete sentences, using appropriate punctuation? It is very important that they use their imagination for the last question!

 Andrew Brodie: More Improving Comprehension for Ages 9–10 © A&C Black, Bloomsbury Publishing 2012

Swimming lesson

Eddie is having a swimming lesson with his teacher, Mr Tuffman. He has become distracted by a loose tile at the bottom of the pool.

This was Eddie's problem. It always happened. It was what made Tuffman so impatient with him. It was what made Tariq so amused by him. He just couldn't concentrate on what he was supposed to be doing when something else had distracted him. On this occasion he was supposed to be collecting the rubber brick but he was distracted by the loose tile. He couldn't stop himself from pausing to pick at it even though, way back up at the surface, Tuffman would be counting away to himself.

What was particularly interesting about the tile was that it looked like it had never been stuck down properly. It was surprisingly big as well – it must have been about forty or fifty centimetres square – but as Eddie glanced around he noticed that all of the tiles were this size. It was definitely loose. And if it was loose, surely that meant you had to lift it up to see what was underneath it?

Eddie lifted it up to see what was underneath it. As soon as he did so he regretted it. The water seemed to suck him very strongly towards the hole that was revealed. It was just like pulling the plug out of the bath then putting your foot over the plug-hole: suction. Extremely powerful suction.

Instinctively, Eddie put his hands out in front of himself but this only served to make him more streamlined and the power of the sucking water pulled him into the swimming pool's plug-hole. He shot through the hole and into a pipe that wound upwards and downwards, left and right, just like the water-chute tube that he had been in on holiday … only better! (If you liked that sort of thing, which he did.) Eddie wanted it to go on forever.

This was so much fun. He forgot his swimming lesson, the brick and, most of all, Mr Tuffman's counting. He simply relaxed and let the water shoot him forward but quite suddenly, he popped out of the tube and found himself in water that was colder than the swimming pool that he had left.

Swimming lesson

1   What lesson is Eddie having?

_____

_____

2   What is Eddie supposed to be doing?

_____

_____

3   What distracted Eddie?

_____

_____

4   What happened when Eddie lifted the tile?

_____

_____

5   Why did Eddie want the journey through the tube to go on forever?

_____

_____

6   Write about a time when you went swimming.

_____

_____

_____

_____

_____

Notes for teachers
Help the children to read the passage slowly and carefully, ensuring that they understand the story. Discuss the questions with them and encourage them to work out their answers orally before putting anything down on paper. Do they remember to write in complete sentences, using appropriate punctuation? Talk about a time when the children went swimming – what can they remember about it?

   Andrew Brodie: More Improving Comprehension for Ages 9–10 © A&C Black, Bloomsbury Publishing 2012

Swimming lesson

1 Who do you think Tariq is?

_____

_____

2 What is special about the tile that Eddie is looking at?

_____

_____

3 Why did Eddie regret lifting the tile?

_____

_____

4 Did he regret it for very long? How did he feel once the first shock was over?

_____

_____

5 What did Eddie forget?

_____

_____

6 Write about a time when you went swimming. Think about one thing that happened that made the occasion a bit special.

_____

_____

_____

_____

_____

Notes for teachers
Ask the children to read the passage carefully, ensuring that they understand the story. Discuss the questions with them and encourage them to work out their answers orally before putting anything down on paper. Do they remember to write in complete sentences, using appropriate punctuation? Talk about a time when the children went swimming – what can they remember about it?

Swimming lesson

1 Apart from Eddie, which other characters are mentioned in the passage?

_____

_____

2 Why was Eddie supposed to be collecting a rubber brick?

_____

_____

3 What was particularly interesting about the tile?

_____

_____

4 What does 'streamlined' mean?

_____

_____

5 How do you feel that Mr Tuffman might react to what Eddie has done?

_____

_____

6 What do you think could happen next in the story? You could continue on a separate sheet if you need to.

_____

_____

_____

_____

_____

Notes for teachers
Ask the children to read the passage carefully, ensuring that they understand the story. Do they remember to write their answers in complete sentences, using appropriate punctuation? Talk about a time when the children went swimming – what can they remember about it? Does this give them any clues for continuing the story?

Andrew Brodie: More Improving Comprehension for Ages 9–10 © A&C Black, Bloomsbury Publishing 2012

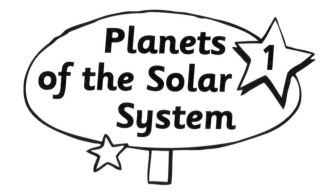

Planets of the Solar System 1

Read these important facts:

- A planet is a celestial body that orbits a star.

- The sun is a star.

- The word solar means 'relating to the sun'.

- The sun is the star at the centre of the solar system.

- The word celestial means 'heavenly' but it also means 'of the sky' or 'of outer space'.

- The word orbit means the path a planet takes to go round a star.

- Gravity is the force that attracts a planet to the star.

- Each planet also has its own gravity.

- Gravity is the force that keeps us on the ground!

- The force of gravity pulls objects towards the ground.

- Scientists tell us that there are eight planets in our solar system.

- We live on the planet Earth.

- The other seven planets in the solar system are Mercury, Venus, Mars, Jupiter, Saturn, Uranus and Neptune.

- Scientists who study space are called astronomers.

- Astronomers used to think that Pluto was a planet.

- The International Astronomical Union decided in 2006 that Pluto is not a planet.

- Pluto is now known as a dwarf planet.

- Another dwarf planet is called Eris.

- Eris is bigger than Pluto.

Planets of the Solar System 1

Name: _____ Date: _____

Some sentences have been split into two parts. Match the two parts of each sentence.

The sun is the star   pulls objects towards the ground.

The force of gravity   that orbits a star.

Scientists who study space   at the centre of the solar system.

A planet is a celestial body   are called astronomers.

Answer these questions using full sentences.

What star is at the centre of the solar system?

_____

_____

_____

On which planet do we live?

_____

_____

_____

What is the name for scientists who study space?

_____

_____

_____

Notes for teachers
The sheet presents a long list of facts from which the pupils need to sift information, a difficult but very useful skill. The pupils will also be meeting new vocabulary and may need help in decoding some of the words. Read through all the facts with the children, helping them to understand each one if possible. Talk through the questions and encourage the pupils to compose full sentences for their answers.

Name: _____ Date: _____

Some sentences have been split into two parts. Match the two parts of each sentence.

The word celestial means   relating to the sun.

The word solar means   of the sky.

Gravity is the force that   Pluto was a planet.

Astronomers used to think that   attracts a planet to a star.

Answer these questions using full sentences.

What does the word orbit mean?

_____

_____

How many planets are there in the solar system?

_____

_____

What do you know about gravity?

_____

_____

_____

_____

Notes for teachers
The sheet presents a long list of facts from which the pupils need to sift information, a difficult but very useful skill. The pupils will also be meeting new vocabulary and may need help in decoding some of the words. Read through all the facts with the children, helping them to understand each one if possible. Talk through the questions and encourage the pupils to compose full sentences for their answers. The final question requires pupils to combine information from the given facts and possibly to add information from other sources.

Planets of the Solar System 1

Some sentences have been split into two parts. Match the two parts of each sentence.

Stars, planets and moons   are two of the planets.

Astronomers tell us that there   are celestial bodies.

Eris and Pluto   are two of the dwarf planets.

Mercury and Venus   are eight planets in the solar system.

Answer these questions using full sentences.

Why are planets and stars known as celestial bodies?

_____

_____

What effects does gravity have?

_____

_____

_____

Write about Pluto. You may wish to find more information such as when it was first discovered.

_____

_____

_____

Notes for teachers
The sheet presents a long list of facts from which the pupils need to sift information, a difficult but very useful skill. The pupils will also be meeting new vocabulary and may need help in decoding some of the words. Read through all the facts with the children, helping them to understand each one if possible. Talk through the questions and encourage the pupils to compose full sentences for their answers. The final two questions require pupils to combine information from the given facts and possibly to add information from other sources.

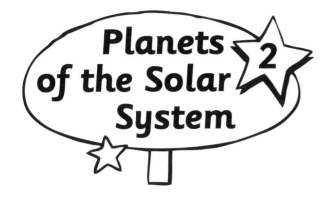

Planets of the Solar System 2

Read these important facts:

- There are eight planets in the solar system.

- There are also at least five dwarf planets in the solar system.

- Astronomers don't know exactly how many dwarf planets there are.

- Pluto is a dwarf planet.

- The eight planets in the solar system, in order of their distance from the sun, are Mercury, Venus, Earth, Mars, Jupiter, Saturn, Uranus and Neptune.

- The planet closest to the sun is Mercury.

- The planet furthest from the sun is Neptune.

- Earth is third closest to the sun.

- Jupiter is the largest planet in the solar system.

- The smallest planet in the solar system is Mercury.

- Four planets are composed mainly of rock and are known as terrestrials.

- The four other planets are known as gas giants.

- Some planets have moons that orbit them.

- Earth has one moon.

- Mars has two moons.

- Jupiter has sixty-four moons.

Planets of the Solar System 2

Use full sentences to answer these questions.

How many planets are there in the solar system?

_____

_____

What type of celestial body is Pluto?

_____

_____

Which two planets are closest to the sun?

_____

_____

Which two planets are furthest from the sun?

_____

_____

How many moons does Earth have?

_____

_____

Write the names of the planets in order of their distance from the sun.

_____

_____

Notes for teachers
This activity should be completed after the pupils have worked on Planets of the Solar System 1. Again, this sheet presents a long list of facts from which the pupils need to sift information, a difficult but very useful skill. The pupils will also be meeting new vocabulary and may need help in decoding some of the words. Read through all the facts with the children, helping them to understand each one if possible. Talk through the questions and encourage the pupils to compose full sentences for their answers.

Name: _____ Date: _____

Use full sentences to answer these questions.

How many planets are there in the solar system?

_____

_____

What other celestial bodies are there in the solar system?

_____

_____

What name is given to planets that consist mainly of rock?

_____

_____

What are the other planets classified as?

_____

_____

Which is the smallest planet in the solar system?

_____

_____

Write the first letter of each planet, in the order of the distances of the planets from the sun. Try to make up a mnemonic to help you to remember the order.

_____

_____

Notes for teachers
This activity should be completed after the pupils have worked on Planets of the Solar System 1. Again, this sheet presents a long list of facts from which the pupils need to sift information, a difficult but very useful skill. Discuss the word mnemonic with the children – do they understand what it is? You may like to give them some examples before they attempt the last question.

Planets of the Solar System ⭐2

Use full sentences to answer these questions.

Why do you think astronomers don't know how many dwarf planets there are?

_____

_____

Write two facts about Mercury.

_____

_____

What celestial body orbits Earth?

_____

_____

What does the name 'gas giants' suggest about four of the planets?

_____

_____

Which of the planets are gas giants? Use your own research skills to find out.

_____

_____

Write the first letter of each planet, in the order of the distances of the planets from the sun. Try to make up a mnemonic to help you to remember the order.

_____

_____

Notes for teachers
This activity should be completed after the pupils have worked on Planets of the Solar System 1. Again, this sheet presents a long list of facts from which the pupils need to sift information, a difficult but very useful skill. Discuss the word mnemonic with the children – do they understand what it is? You may like to give them some examples before they attempt the last question.

Preparatory Test

FROM 1990 UNTIL FURTHER NOTICE

Cello

The Associated Board of the Royal Schools of Music

PREPARATORY TEST: CELLO

1 The candidate will be asked to play the following exercises from memory.

(a) For bow arm levels with free wrist for string crossings.

(b) For creating an even tone, with smooth joins, and thinking of bow speed.

(c) For correct finger spacing, making sure fingers are rounded and playing on finger tips, keeping fingers down.

AB 2126

Variations on an Unoriginal Theme

TERENCE GREAVES

3   Own choice

The candidate should bring a short piece of his/her own choice to play. The piano accompaniment will be played by the examiner, and candidates must ensure that the piano part is brought to the examination. The candidate will be required to indicate to the examiner the speed of the piece by either tapping the beat or playing the opening two or three bars.

4 **The candidate will be asked to respond to the following tests.**

(a) The examiner will play, one after the other, two widely-spread notes on the piano, within the range of three octaves. The candidate will be asked to state which is the higher note (first or second). The examiner will then play a note within the voice range which the candidate will be asked to sing.

(b) The examiner will tap a rhythm which the candidate will be asked to imitate as an echo. The candidate should tap the echo in time immediately after the examiner. Two further rhythms will follow on without a break, as illustrated below.

Example

(c) The examiner will play a piece on the piano in 2 or 3 time, and the candidate will be asked to join in as soon as possible by tapping the beat, indicating where the strong beat falls.

Example

Reproduced and printed by
Halstan & Co. Ltd., Amersham, Bucks., England   AB 2126

The Associated Board of
the Royal Schools of Music
(Publishing) Limited

14 Bedford Square
London WC1B 3JG

ISBN 1-85472-497-5

ALFRED'S BASIC
MANDOLIN METHOD
1

..... THE MOST POPULAR METHOD
FOR LEARNING HOW TO PLAY

For individual or class instruction ....

RON MANUS & L. C. HARNSBERGER

TnT²
SOFTWARE
VIDEO AUDIO
ONLINE ACCESS
INCLUDED

Alfred

REVISED EDITION